# JUST CALL ME SPAZ

To people confused and frightened about what life
with epilepsy may hold for them.

You can achieve your dreams.

# ACKNOWLEDGMENTS

Thank you to Randy, Debbie, Cheryl and Ron, staff of Staircase Teen Shelter, which unfortunately no longer operates in Ludington, MI. I have fond memories of my time spent there.

Thank you to Peggy Byland, the editor of tc Street Voices, a non-profit organization in Traverse City, MI, who edited my work and guided this book to completion. Tc Street Voices gives writing opportunities to people impacted by poverty.

Thank you to a generous donor who contributed funds for the publishing of this book. Thanks to Mission Point Press who made it possible to put this book into your hands.

Thanks to Dan and the morning crew girls at Traverse City Big Boy for that extra push to realize my dream of writing a book. The coffee helped, too!

David (3rd from left) with brother Bob, sister
Audrey and Cousin Leslie.

# CHAPTER 1

Everyone goes down his or her own road through life. One person's life may seem dark and dreary, while another person seems to be living a bright and exciting life. Yet, some folks live by ways and means that are far from either. Your "Average Joe" is a man who doesn't have everything he needs to live his life to the fullest. Instead, "Joe" struggles to gain or stay ahead or to maintain his status quo, feeling proud of the things he's accomplished. THAT is kind of like me.

I am an epileptic. The seizures I experience are defined as "partial-complex." But, I still don't know much about my illness. When I was nine, doctors identified a small scar on my brain, located just behind my left ear, and determined that is the cause of my epilepsy.

The most common seizure I experience is called petite mal. But I also go through a grand mal seizure every now and then. Grand mal seizures include bad convulsions as well.

That's one experience I don't like to face, and lucky me, I don't have to face those episodes very often. I am familiar with these types of seizures, but as far as different types of epilepsy, the list is endless.

Today, 45 years after my first seizure, I can give a description of a petit mal seizure. To me it's like this: the seizure starts in the diaphragm, the feelings through my body start to take over and, within seconds, it's a whole new world, or a whole new realm. An "aura," as doctors call it, is a different world in itself. I've noticed its length of time seems to be determined by the strength or severity of the seizure and atmospheric conditions.

An "aura" experience could be more accurately described like an automobile. After each seizure, I can sit and idle with no problem. The hard part is, I can't seem to get my clutch to put me back in gear.

But, there are some differences between them, also. For instance, at the beginning of a seizure, many start light and then, gradually glide through to their highest "potency." Others may be lighter and brief. Just a quick come and go. In my dictionary, those are "Floaters."

Stronger seizures hit me harder and make me work more trying to avoid them, or maybe try to dodge them. As in that automobile example, this time, when those gears and the clutch are doing their job, they pop out of place, starting a stronger feeling aura.

Today, my seizures still begin in my diaphragm, feeling like a light shock of electricity followed by that new or "different realm" type of atmosphere, although the new development I noticed, lately, is a strong urge to cry. The stronger the seizure, the more crying I'll experience. At my age, that is difficult to deal with.

David, age 9.

# CHAPTER 2

I can only describe my first seizure experience as a blur. I remember a minor petit mal seizure occurred when I was nine. My family and I were watching the popular television show, "Mutual of Omaha's Wild Kingdom." It was a family affair we all loved. My siblings and I would get lost in the program. Mom loved it, too.

As the kids sat there, Mom was sitting quietly nearby, making it a restful, relaxing time for her as well. Mom knew to take advantage of that whenever possible. But, that was going to be one episode of "Wild Kingdom" that I will never forget. During that episode, something happened to me. The whole show suddenly seemed different. I remember the scenes of the documentary at the time, but the atmosphere I was in seemed to be different. There was a weird feeling in my diaphragm, but no pain at all. It was a strange experience. It didn't last for long, and nobody in the family knew what had just happened, but me.

My first grand mal seizure, to my knowledge, occurred when my family and friends were perch fishing on Portage Lake, in Onekama, Michigan. We decided to bring the boat in to enjoy a picnic. While the adults got the picnic ready, I led the kids to the water to catch crayfish for bait. All was good. The bait bucket was filling up.

I was climbing on top of a boulder in the shallow water at the shore, when I began to feel that light shock feeling in my diaphragm. That's all I can remember. The kids reported I fell from the boulder and sank to the bottom of the lake. Although I don't recall any of that happening, my mother told me, "It all happened so fast."

Our friend Jim was the first to respond, running to the water and dragging me out onto the grass alongside the shoreline. Some people remember my efforts to get away from the paramedics. Mom told me I seemed to be frozen stiff. The medics strapped me to the stretcher and gave me a free ride to the hospital. Very scary at the time!

Of course, to a young kid, that was an abrupt introduction to what became a life-changing experience. Although many have common factors, some of my memories of the seizures are only a blur. From that day forward, my young life was constant visits to the University of Michigan Hospital's Department of Neurology and the Talbaum Children's Center for a variety of tests, namely EEGs and MRIs, among many others I cannot recall. The doctors put me on Phenobarbital, a memorable experience in itself. Do remember, I was only in grade school!

My junior high school years offered a new beginning—new building, new students and teachers, new expectations—a different world entirely!

As I entered the seventh grade, I began playing the trumpet in the Brethern Junior High band. That was when the seizures became more frequent.

In junior high school, kids my age avoided the older students. However, one way or another, they would find us. Peer pressure introduced me to cigarettes at the age of thirteen. The boys' bathroom, or as it was called back then, the "john," was a place of relative safety from older students and teachers, male and female. Stepping into the john, you were greeted with a heavy cloud of smoke. If the teachers found you smoking, you would be the next one to get suspended for three days PLUS 20 hours of study hall.

Throughout my school years, I had a bundle of seizures that became too much of a burden for me. Soon I was trying to avoid the possibilities of those seizures happening in a public place. School no longer seemed important; it didn't seem to matter. I was more interested in knowing more about my disease and finding a new life. That's what got me my walking papers—walking right into Camp Shawano, the boys' detention center, AKA boot camp.

At Camp Shawano residents agreed to and signed the rules and regulations the minute they walked in the door. If not, you could plan on spending your time in the county jail.

# CHAPTER 3

At Camp Shawano, I began to experience and enjoy the new world of cooking—and the kitchen warfare that came with it. KP wasn't bad. In fact, it was much better than getting assigned a work position in the Forestry Division. Every day, that gang travelled all over, on highways, roads, even snowmobile trails. They went to barns and warehouses to make, paint and detail signs. From what the guys told me, the gang spent a lot of time traveling to replace many damaged and aging signs. Some of them loved it, so they said.

My job in the camp kitchen was similar in some ways: rise at 5 a.m., shower, and get to the cafeteria building on time. Be late and you had to answer to "Smitty," the chef, organizer, supervisor and—when necessary—the enforcer. Smitty took boys to the "tool shed," a somewhat scary event from what I heard.

In addition, every day came with assigned studies for the completion of your GED. The last thing you needed was to have Smitty piling extra cleanup or preparations or set-up. Smitty was someone you knew you had to respect. If Smitty said to do something you did it—fast! No questions asked, no delay either. Staying on Smitty's good side was a goal all boys aimed to accomplish! Smitty was someone with a firm fist!

After about six months, I got a phone call from my caseworker at Manistee County Department of Social Services, telling me that I was going to a different place to complete the GED. He said it was Staircase, a home-like, halfway house in Ludington, Michigan, with a different, more relaxing atmosphere.

Of course, I was all for it. I started missing Smitty right away...NOT!

On my first day at Staircase, possibly called that because of the huge flight of stairs between floors, I explored the building with a very attractive director's assistant. It was then I realized just how enormous Staircase was. There were classrooms, study rooms, a living room, a huge dining room and the kitchen, pantry and laundry room. Down in the basement there was the recreation room with a pool table, exercise mats and more health equipment. To many of us, heaven was in the stereo room. Most of us spent a lot of free time in the stereo room listening to music—at a realistic volume, of course.

Up on the third floor were all the bedrooms and bathrooms. Judy, the director's assistant, showed me to my room and told me to unpack and make myself at home. Then she went back down to the main floor, to her office.

After I got most of my belongings put away and organized the shelves in the closet, I decided it was time to do a more thorough investigation of the place.

Surprising enough, I only made it to the top of the stairs, took two steps down, when all of a sudden, I heard, "Hey, Stendel, what are you doing here? On my first day as a resident in Staircase, I never expected to run into a junior high school classmate. Good 'ole Tim Foster, my bodyguard through the first years in junior high school, even after the introduction to seizures. We updated each other on our lives since we left public school and looked back to a couple of pranks we pulled on our previous teachers. Then we recalled an incident that we both could never forget.

That happened when we played on the school band. Tim reminded me, "During a class session, Mr. Wave (band director), got a big surprise. We were playing that Carpenter song. I don't remember the name of it but I could sing it to you," he said with a laugh.

"When that 'spaz'(seizure) took over," Tim said, "Mr. Wave got a little nervous. He called Eckhart (the principal at the time), who called your folks."

That's about where I can vaguely remember Mr. Wave telling my mother that the reason I was having those seizures was because "playing the trumpet was putting too much pressure to the head." That's when he made me start playing the baritone instead. I still wonder what's the difference?

Tim then added, "Yeah, when you had that seizure, I remember I grabbed the horn and tossed it aside so you wouldn't hurt yourself. After it was over and your Mom came to take you home, Mr. Wave called me into his office. He was going to charge me for the minor damage to the horn. I called him a bad word and walked out. I was done with that."

Tim and I both laughed about it and Tim started telling me of another time I had a severe grand mal seizure, not long after that one.

One morning at school, the two of us headed into the john to have a cigarette before the bell rang. Just as we began, in walked two seniors who made it a habit to beat and assault younger students. I guess it made them proud. Little did they know, they were about to get a surprise, a BIG one they would never forget.

Tim was getting pounded and I was threatened to a 'royal flush,' when I felt the beginning of a petit mal seizure. Evidently, that seizure soon turned into a full blown Grand Mal seizure. That was the last thing I remember.

Tim then continued with the rest of the story. He said, "You should've seen the faces on those two. The moment you fell to the floor, they both turned pale. When Mr. Thomas and Mr. Phillips got the news, they both came to help and immediately took you to the nurses' lounge.

Eckhardt, the Principal at that time, dragged Spoor and Weaver off to his office. They were on the edge of their chairs. They looked in to see if you were still moving. They were whiter than ghosts; they thought you were dead. It was the funniest thing ever," Foster said.

Later that same day, I started meeting some more of the staff members at Staircase. First was Cheryl. She was small, thin and cute. She seemed outspoken and pretty easy-going at the same time. She helped the residents with counseling when they needed it, and gave input on solving the many problems that constantly developed throughout the week. Her smile and upbeat attitude gave me a whole new perspective on why I was at Staircase (and the possibilities for success while there).

The next staff member was Debbie, sort of our "housemother" and teacher. She was one staff who lived at Staircase. Frankly, I don't know how she survived. She took quite a bit of stress-related punishment from us kids. Still, when study hour was in session, Debbie was at her desk, ready and willing to help us in locating items we needed to find answers to questions pertaining to any subject. But, Debbie never gave the actual answer. She would direct us to where and advise on how to search for the answer. "That's not my job. Studying is an accomplishment you do yourself." Then she would point us to the right bookshelf.

Randy was our house father. He had his own bedroom and was often an overnight staff. He did a lot of activities the residents were interested in, from playing pool to going to the community college just outside of Ludington. Randy and Debbie both took us to the college, one day each week, for a variety of recreational activities—dodge-ball, basketball, volleyball, or swimming in the college pool.

Randy was like a big brother to me. Some residents would want to go to the movies or the beach. I'd try to talk Randy into going fishing—and that wasn't hard. We did quite a bit of fishing. We'd go to different lakes and streams for catching, or trying to catch, many different species of fish. Steelhead, salmon (coho and Chinook), and muskellunge were at the top of our list of fish, depending on the season. We did get our share of each, bringing freshly-caught fish back to the House which eventually lead to a 'scrumptious' fish fry.

Of course, Debbie had to give me permission to go. I remember once, Randy met me at the front door with the idea of going salmon fishing. We grabbed our poles and were almost out the door. Then Debbie interrupted our intentions. Truth is, I was whining so much that I had to make a deal with her to get her to okay our plan. We decided to add an extra half-hour to my daily study time every time we made plans to go fishing. That was a pretty good deal to me. One half-hour of extra studying for three, maybe four hours of fishing. You do the math. For me, fishing always came first and Deb knew it.

A nice Chinook.

# CHAPTER 4

One bright, sunny day, Randy, a neighbor "mascot" nicknamed Jay-bird, and I with a packed lunch and all the necessities, headed to the pier on Lake Michigan to fish for salmon. On the pier, we noticed a bunch of fishermen, men and women both, lined up on the side shelf of the pier, facing the lighthouse. We came up to an older couple with Chinook, a few Coho salmon and a couple brown trout—eight to be exact! As Randy talked to them, we found out the man's wife caught all eight! No words can describe the look on the man's face. No one wants to say anything when out-fished by their spouse—especially a husband!

The next thing I remember is waking up to unfamiliar faces trying to get my attention. An emergency paramedic was trying to get me back to reality. Later, Randy told me I'd had another seizure and luckily, the man's wife carried a phone in her purse (that wasn't as common, then, as it is today—and the phone was huge!). Anyway, the ambulance took me to the hospital where doctors gave me blood tests and put me on observation for a while. Eventually, Randy, Jay-bird and I headed back to Staircase —with no fish.

Back at Staircase, I was exhausted and so went straight to my room. For the next few days, many residents asked me what I remembered about what happened. "What was the problem," I thought. "What's wrong with me?" I was anxious to find out.

As timed passed, so did the doctor appointments. For a while it seemed like an everyday event—MRIs, CTs, and EEGs—until it got to seem like a medical alphabet system. Eventually I really didn't care. Still none of it made any sense. From then on, my life seemed to be an everlasting blur.

However, I do recall the lovable Theresa. She was a new resident in Staircase who was studying to take the S.A.T. She was determined to get into Michigan State University. Theresa and I hit it off on day one. And to me she was like a sweet aroma in the air at Staircase.

When Theresa stepped into Staircase, she brought a bright rainbow into my life. She was someone I could talk to when I had to get the epilepsy thing out of my head. She, too, was studying to finish her GED and was looking forward to going to MSU in lower Michigan. When she needed to quiz herself, in any subject, I was available to help.

At times, when others were going to special events, Theresa and I would go down to the harbor and lay out a blanket. Watching the sunset over Lake Michigan gave us the enjoyment of serenity. Our time together seemed ineffable—breathtaking, marvelous, amazing. Our relationship gradually grew. Affection grew strong between us and, in a way, I found the meaning of "first love."

Inevitably things change over time. The time came when Theresa relocated. That was the last thing I wanted to hear. Theresa moved to a dormitory in East Lansing, near Michigan State University. Her departure broke my heart. Staircase seemed pretty empty without her. I did receive a few letters from her, but after a while, we lost contact. I still wonder if she remembers me like I remember her.

As autumn changed to winter, Staircase began to settle down as well. Soon, the activities and recreation nights were limited. Tourist season came to an end, and many small, local businesses closed up until the next spring.

Most outdoor recreation could not continue when snow fell. Basketball and indoor swimming at the college pool were what most of us looked forward to. But once winter blew in and the local lakes were frozen with safe solid ice, Randy and I put out the fish shanty on Hamlin Lake. There we spent mornings and evenings spearing pike and muskellunge. Each trip was mysterious and exciting. We never brought home whoppers, but they were all trophies!

As time went by, I finished my GED. I barely remember leaving Staircase, but believe me, in my heart, Staircase will always be "home."

# CHAPTER 5

The time came for me to go out on my own. At that time, the idea to travel seemed interesting, and a journey across the United States sounded a little exciting. Why not!? I was done with school, and visiting different regions in the United States, observing their cultures and ways of living, would be something very new to me. Who knows? I could begin a new life in a whole different place.

It was the end of the 1970s when I hit the road. I was a 17-year-old. At that time, people created many interesting ways of travel, including a much cheaper way —hitchhiking. From northern Michigan, I opted for the Interstate Highway South, destination unknown. Meeting new people of many different origins, I began learning about the United States, more than I even realized.

Leaving Ludington, in northern lower Michigan, took nearly a full day of hitching rides to get to Grand Rapids. It was a bit less than 120 miles to a small truck stop where semi-truck drivers refueled, ate and slept,

Ice fishing on Hamlin Lake.

First view of the mountains.

if they were not running behind schedule. There, I caught a ride to Topeka, Kansas.

As soon as the trucker and I left the truck stop, he began asking a lot of questions about the territory where I came from. He told me that he was actually from Carbondale, Kansas, a little way south of Topeka. He also recounted many of his experiences on the road, and advised me on what I should know when hitchhiking.

For example, the driver explained that hitchhiking with a truck driver depended on which drivers you asked. The big manufacturers kept strict rules and regulations. He advised me that "there's a slim chance of getting a ride with them" and that "independent truckers" are your best shot. Their driving is much like the "basics," but they are their own boss. Riding with independent truckers helped me cover many miles and catch up on my sleep.

Sometimes there was even an odd job or two. Loading and unloading cargo was an experience in itself.

My first episode of epilepsy on the road was another surprise. I recall getting a ride from a woman named Carla, a graduate of a culinary school in South Dakota, who, at that time, was attempting to open her own restaurant/truck stop on an interstate highway, just north of Sioux Falls, Iowa. Carla regaled me with her stories of getting her project launched and I told her about Camp Shawano.

During our ride, Carla asked if I was interested in an hourly job, helping her to open her place more quickly. She also offered me a clean room for dirt cheap. As I had no place in particular to go and my timetable was my own, I accepted. I realized that my time in the kitchen at Camp Shawano would be put to good use! However, the first day proved a little shaky.

As Carla introduced me to her kitchen, I had a seizure—right in front of her. Carla was describing what she decided to put on the menu and all that she accomplished to date. Wham! Out of the blue, I fell off the chair and landed flat on my back.

Carla was sympathetic and familiar with epilepsy and its recurrences. She told me that her younger sister also lived with epilepsy, describing some of her bad seizure experiences. She told me that my episode was not severe when compared to her sister's. I was relieved to hear her story. Carla suggested I lie down, which sounded great to me, at that time, and that we could continue our running later.

After a relaxing two hours, Carla and I hit the road again, headed to pick up restaurant supplies. One stop was a small roadside farm market where we purchased a flat of jumbo-sized blackberries—literally an inch in diameter! We also bought four, 100-pound bags of potatoes and other assorted vegetables for Carla's opening specials. She set up the delivery day and then we left.

Downtown Boulder, CO, Pearl St. Mall

On our way back, we stopped at an elderly lady's rummage sale. We learned her husband had passed away and she decided to get rid of some of his things, like clothes, tools and miscellaneous stuff.

Carla bought me a nice Stetson hat—a big surprise that fit great!

Back at the restaurant, I started washing the berries, freezing many for later. I used the last of the berries for pies—another opening day treat!

The kitchen was the last thing we were worried about. In the dining room, we put in new dining room tables and booths along the walls. We even put in an ice cream freezer with pie shelves to advertise the pies and any other desserts we decided to make later

When we opened the restaurant doors, we did more business than we ever expected. We were both so proud of our accomplishments—of course the real credit goes straight to Carla. By the day's end, we were ready for a little celebration and so we treated each other to a night on the town—nothing spectacular, really just a pat on the back, and right back to it first thing next morning.

I helped Carla with the truck stop for just over four months staying until she was comfortable and had hired a couple more people willing to put in some long and busy days. While time with Carla and her start-up was fun, I decided to continue on with my nationwide "vacation." To this day, I still need "a good kick in the pants" for leaving such a great place.

# CHAPTER 6

From Sioux Falls, South Dakota, I continued south a short distance to I-29, on my way to Colorado! Within two days, I found myself at Pearl Street Mall, in the heart of Boulder, Colorado, a home for a lot of college "yuppie" students.

Boulder was also the home to the television show, "Mork and Mindy." I lived by the original house used for taping the show! However, within a few months, a chain link fence was installed to keep people from stealing things. I even heard that parts of the house's toilet went missing!

At this time, my older brother Bob was in the US Marine Corps Band. Bobby could play a variety of instruments. As a matter of fact, Bobby played for the inauguration of President Ronald Reagan! He was proud…and so was Mom. Bobby was stationed at Camp Pendleton, in San Diego, California. My visit with my brother Bob taught me one thing in particular; doing time in the US Military Services surely was not for me.

Somehow the next leg of my journey led me right back to the same region in northwestern lower Michigan, but to the bigger town of Traverse City. Still, I cannot say that the hitchhiking ended there. For a long time, my only way of travel was hitchhiking. If I wanted to reach any destination outside of Traverse City, I was hitchhiking.

People of the area were now starting to hear more bad news about hitchhiking and the majority of drivers would think twice before offering someone any travel assistance. There were some scary reports that put an end to hitchhiking for good.

# CHAPTER 7

When I got back to Traverse City, I called my Aunt Velma at her family farm where she raised her family, and I learned that my father was staying with her. Dad, at that time, was going through a severe case of depression. I can remember when I and all my siblings were very young, Dad had experienced a few things that really hurt him emotionally, and sometimes so severe that he acted like he was mentally ill.

My father was injured when he in the navy. He had a hard time, disabled and with too much time on his hands. He wasn't in a wheelchair or anything like that, but the after effect of his injury did have some part in his emotional disabilities. My father and I stayed with my Aunt Velma for a good amount of time, pretty much until we decided to move to a neighborhood in the heart of Traverse City.

In Traverse City, I remember trying to hold a job simultaneous with experiencing seizures. I recall being employed at Holiday Inn, inside at Shimmers Lounge, with the position of prep cook. My job description also included serving as a chef's assistant, slicing huge and perfectly cooked roasts for guests and businesses during Happy Hour, 4:00-8:30 p.m. I kept serving tables stocked with vegetable trays and side salads, both pickled and creamy herring, tuna casserole and rolls. It was fun!

Most of all, I loved Monday Night Football, when in season. During the games, I served hot dogs, hamburgers, and draft beers—plus waiting on tables. Half-times were quite busy. Customers ordered more drinks and the tips got bigger! I sometimes discovered that the tip left was not the amount intended. A customer might leave a couple of bucks on the table. When I cleared the tables, I'd just stuff the tips in my pocket and carry on cleaning. Later, behind the bar, I was often surprised to discover that a "couple of bucks" were actually two ten dollar bills. One time, I found that people left a twenty, a five, and two ones. Lord knows that wasn't intentional—but well appreciated!

As I headed to Munson Medical Center on my way to a blood test, I had a seizure and, as I recall I tried to pull over. But minutes later, when I woke up from the seizure, two police officers were getting my attention, trying to get me to answer questions like, "What's your name, who's the president," and the funniest one, "Have you been drinking?"

When I finally came to, I noticed my pick-up truck was crashed, face-to-face with another man's truck, in his back yard, right in front of his garage. And from all the evidence, I came coasting off the street, knocked down a chain-link fence next to the man's yard, and somehow, rolled right in on the guy's driveway. I have to be truthful, I really felt sorry for the owner of the truck. A new truck already ruined.

I'm glad I had insurance and was totally covered, but as soon as everything was all over, I gave up driving. That was 34 years ago. I bet the insurance company was more than glad to let me go!

# CHAPTER 8

There was a long time that was quite "cloudy." For much of that time I was visiting doctors, seeking help to tame those seizures of mine. Different doctors with different tests were a little easier to recognize, for example EEG and MRI. Then came sleep tests and others like the "Wada" test.

As I recall, for the Wada test a catheter was inserted into a main artery to measure the flow of blood to my brain, at least that was my understanding of the test. Anyway, the doctors had me look at a line of pictures and then asked me to describe the subject on each card—which they told me I described correctly. Then they performed the same procedure again, putting the same drug into the opposite side of my brain.

What a difference! The doctors reported that the effect on the second side immediately made me seem to be, in my word, a vegetable, totally unaware of what was happening. I had no response to the cards.

Following the Wada tests, the neurologist recommended that I consider head surgery. When they started talking about the surgery, they said they had to inform me of all of the types of possibilities that could result from the neuro-surgery. At the start, they told me that the ratio of getting rid of the epilepsy, totally, was 97%. That sounded pretty good at first. But that's just the beginning. For the next nine months I had appointments, over and over, to keep the information they needed updated. The tests seemed as if they were getting longer and longer. I began to notice that the 97% ratio began to get lower and lower. The next neuro-surgeon gave me the ratio of 85% chance of some impairment. But, that's where they threw in the possibilities of......DEATH!! That threw a wrench into the gears!

No way was I going to play the role of a guinea pig. "I can live with the epilepsy," I thought to myself. The brain surgery was not going to happen. Not for me, anyway. From that day forward, the answer for me is that I can live with it. In addition, I may donate my brain upon death to the medical field, but I still have a long way to go...and I'm going as Me!

After this, my doctors tried many different drugs for controlling my seizures. At the start, they had me on small, daily dosages of Phenobarbital. When the Phenobarbital was considered in full effect, my attitude was very "touchy," and I had a bad habit of losing my temper. I have to say it wasn't fun. Time and again, I had blood tests and felt like a pin cushion.

For quite some time, doctors had me on the Phenobarbital. But now they put Dilantin into the picture. Two anti-depressants used to slow down my seizures. But never would they eliminate my seizures permanently. After a while, the Phenobarbital and Dilantin seemed to lose their effectiveness. That's when the doctors decided to add Tegretol 200mg. That was a good idea. At first, it wasn't really much of a help, but the Tegretol was increased a little at a time, and slowly made my maintenance of the seizures more manageable.

I was now taking two daily doses of Phenobarbital, and Dilantin, and Tegretol 200mg: 1 tablet a.m. and 1 in the evening. That was then increased to 2 tabs, a.m. and p.m. Still the increases continued. The whole time the doctors were adding Tegretol, they slowly started to decrease, and soon eliminate the Phenobarbital. Next was the elimination of the Dilantin. It's been shown, a steady intake of Dilantin can do some damage to the kidneys and also the liver. So, they started me on another drug called Lamictal, taking the Dilantin out of the picture, as well.

After that, it was differing lengths of time increasing the dosages, until it came to be a balance beneficial for my seizure control. To this day, my seizures still exist, but with the combinations of Tegretol 400XR, 1tablet a.m., 2 tablets p.m., along with Lamictal 200mg, 2 tabs a.m. and 2 p.m., it's been some help to me in a number of ways.

# CHAPTER 9

**A**t 54, I'm more than satisfied with the results of my drug regimen. A lot of my family and friends seem to be surprised I'm still here, given all the different episodes and even traumas I've experienced. When I reminisce, there are quite a few incidents that seem hard to believe. Yet, most of them came with some foolish performances of some sort that to me, ended with a laugh.

For instance, I was doing some work with the Big Boy Restaurant in Traverse City, back in the nineties, when I flabbergasted almost everyone, customers and co-workers alike. As I was waiting to pick up a paycheck, I helped myself to a cup of coffee and sat down in a booth fit for two people. I then started to talk to an elderly couple at the table next to me, only a divider between us.

After talking with them for a short time, Wendy, their waitress came out with their orders.

Wendy then passed by me to help someone cash out at the register. However, Wendy told me a different version of the incident, with others to back up her story.

The parts of the "activity" I can remember starts with having coffee, and yes, talking with the couple. Suddenly, I felt the beginning of a seizure. I started to feel the intense, but definitely painless, changes that occur as I get farther into the episode. But that's where the story comes to an end. And that's where Wendy's version of the story picks up.

Wendy says, "When the couple started eating, you began drinking your coffee, and then it seemed like you slid off your seat. Immediately you stood up and sat back down in your booth. But, everything you did after that was unbelievable! You stood right up at your table, reached over the divider and grabbed half of the lady's sandwich, took a bite and dropped it back down on her plate." After the seizure was gone, the lady said I even gave her a smile—with a mouthful!

The next thing I recall is walking down the street with Police Officer Dennis Finch, of the Traverse City Police Department, to my apartment. I felt guilty about what I had done and decided to pay for the couple's dinners.

When we got back to the Big Boy, I tried my hardest to apologize, feeling like a fool. The couple said they understood what had happened and why. Since then, Big Boy colleagues have brought this incident up a few times and it seems to get funnier every time. I don't remember a thing.

Since then, I have experienced a multiple number of seizures and, again, probably twice as many I don't recall. Yet, most of the ones I do recall don't seem to have anything in common. Experiencing that new realm, or aura, is never the same. The seizure, in itself, doesn't happen with any consistency, nor is the severity ever the same.

I could go without a seizure for a couple of weeks. Then one begins and slowly develops feeling light. Sometimes they even feel lighter, but, are at a more "come and go faster" tempo. I've noticed also that I experience that type of seizure more around the natural changes of the seasons. But the majority are hard to predict. And again, the strength is at random.

There have been times also, when a seizure actually hit me out of the blue, with not one clue that it was about to begin. Those are the ones that came instantly, leaving me with more after-affects and scaring the "begeebees" out of the people around at that time. I don't have any idea of what it looked like to them, but, little do they know, I end up with a "blank" conscience and a battle trying to maintain my previous activities.

One incident I will never forget changed my desire for hunting from a tree stand, and caused me to sell all my deer hunting equipment—bows, ladders, stands, etc. It not only left a huge question on my life's purpose, but left neuro-surgeons bewildered, also.

# CHAPTER 10

It was December 11, 2010, the second day of muzzle-loading season, and it had been snowing throughout the night, leaving a four to five-inch blanket of freshly fallen snow.

Once the snow ended, the clouds drifted on and clear sky donated a heavy layer of frost on top of the snow —a chilly morning to wake up to.

Walking out to my tree stand that morning seemed to take only half the time, but the trek was very quiet and quite bright before daylight.

I arrived at my stand and immediately noticed dirt had been kicked up on top of the new fallen snow, and deer tracks were all over the area. It had to have been a recent activity since everything else was covered in white. I started up the ladder to my stand, and got set up quickly, locking my body harness to the tree and securely snugging the strap around my body.

Then I began pulling up my gun rope with all my

equipment attached. When everything was disconnected from the line, I put my gun across some branches, sturdy enough to provide a gun rest an arm length away.

Now was coffee time. Thank the Lord for the thermos!

Suddenly, I noticed something coming down the deer trail on the opposite side of my blind. A red fox was in search of an early morning breakfast, claiming his position on nature's food chain. I wished him the best of luck.

Shortly after the peak of sunlight, when I started feeling the cold chill of daybreak slowly finding its way to my bones, I decided to get down and follow those tracks down the deer trail to try an ambush, if anything.

When I was safely on the ground, I took my gun off the rope and started down the runway, about forty yards or so, until it seemed I should get back. So, I slowly and quietly started back toward my blind.

Little did I know my whole life was about to change drastically.

I climbed back up my ladder to my stand and pulled my gun rope up laying my gun across those cedar branches until suddenly my hunting expedition was interrupted by an epileptic seizure.

Now I do remember trying to lock my safety harness, but evidently the seizure took over before I could fully secure it.

All I remember after that is opening my eyes to the bright glare of sunlight shining in my face as I lay there flat on my back looking up at my tree stand.

In my attempt to get up off the ground, I felt a sharp pain throughout my neck and shoulders. The result was obvious. After falling fifteen feet or more, I had some type of serious injury.

Slowly, I made my way back onto my feet, and after what seemed to have been an endless route over stumps and fallen cedar trees, about fifty yards, or so, I finally got to the side of the highway. I knelt down and gradually lowered my body onto the top of a snow bank. Although far from painless, I finally got myself in a more comfortable position.

The next thing I recall was a man's voice asking, "Hey, buddy, are you alright? Is there something I can do?"

I told him what had happened and all I could about my apparent condition and pains. I told him of my cell phone inside my shirt pocket. When he found my phone, he immediately dialed 911 and was talking to someone instantly. He told them of our location. Another car had pulled over before he hung up.

The two people in that car were two registered nurses that had just got off their shift working at Munson

Medical Center in Traverse City, Michigan…a coincidence or what?

They knew just what they should do, too. In no time at all, one of them was keeping me alert, asking me all kinds of questions and keeping me in a conversation, while the other was taking my basic vitals: blood pressure, heart beat, temperature, etc. all before the ambulance and paramedics arrived.

I really don't remember much after that. But, the next thing I do recall is waking up in a hospital bed, sitting not lying with some metal contraption resting on my shoulders. It seemed to be "bolted" or "screwed," literally, into my skull in four different places. A nurse that was in the room told me the contraption was called a "halo," and then she began describing what its purpose was. She said it was a traction device used for stabilization of broken bones in the neck, installed during, or immediately after neck surgeries.

A few minutes later, four doctors came into the room and told me the injury I had was called a "cervical fracture." Then they told me what the "neuro" surgeons did to fix it.

One of the doctors continued to explain: "There are seven cervical vertebrae in the human neck. They're named C-1 through C-7. They help support the neck, holding up the head, allowing us to bend and twist our necks many different ways. Importantly, C-1 through C-7 support and protect our spinal cords.

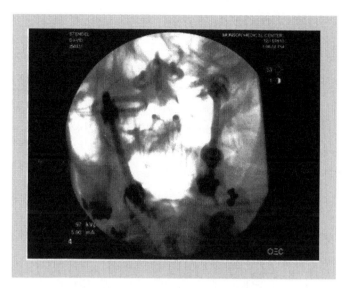

Fusion of vertebrae C-1 and C-2, Top-view, Skull.

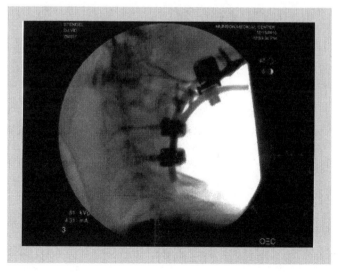

Fusion of vertebrae C-1 and C-2, Side-view, Neck.

Any damage done to the spinal cord can result in severe and even permanent cases of paralysis, sometimes even death."

I found out later, the damage done to my neck was at C-1 and C-2 vertebrae, the first two located at the base of our skull. The doctors also told me they couldn't believe I made it all the way out to the road without doing more damage.

Since that day, I have been introduced to a whole new world of feelings that have come with the trauma, from sudden crying, like I've never experienced before, and new types of pain and new emotions I never knew existed. Some are hard to describe at times.

Now don't get the wrong idea. I support anyone looking forward to the world of hunting in the great outdoors. I only want the younger generation to keep in mind to play it safe and keep coming back. With the practice of previous planning, mixed in some with common sense, you'll realize that to get all the enjoyment of the nature outdoors it will definitely take "Safety First: No Exceptions!"

# CHAPTER 11

Today, a larger number of people believe that each person has his/her destiny. In other words, there is a place in this society for everyone, even though for many that place is not the destiny most of us actually deserve. While the majority of us work harder to achieve what we wish to accomplish, there will always be others who get most of their so-called 'achievements' dropped in their hands after that previous generation achieved it for them. Of course, those are the ones who look down on the part of society not as fortunate as themselves bringing up the many different rumors and stereo-types that exist in our society today.

Still, I've decided to believe the cliché, "Everyone in this world was put here for a purpose.

And, although most of us are struggling today to find out just what his/her purpose may be, I've also found that the more we work toward accomplishing what we feel is right, the better our results will be, even when the result is in our own hearts.

The reason I'm sharing this with you is, if you or someone close to you have what is categorized as a "disease," you will do yourself a favor by not letting others tell you the things you can and cannot do. Everybody will want to put in their words of opinion. Don't let people direct your life. Whether it's what they think you should be doing, or things that they think you shouldn't be doing, or just their personal advice, do not let them discourage you from achieving your goals only because THEY think it's not safe. It is far more beneficial to consider taking serious thought to what your doctors and neurologists advise you to do, especially if you are having an overwhelming amount of seizures and conditions that may cause you more harm and injuries. It is much safer and easier to take your time and get help from the medical advances that have been discovered in the last century. It can give you a great number of benefits when all is accomplished with an understanding everyone can relate to.

I'm glad to say that I've noticed lately the younger generation has a better understanding of what epilepsy is. They can accept many of their acquaintances who have epilepsy and, most of all, are willing to learn the facts toward assisting someone who does experiences epileptic seizures. As I mentioned earlier, no two people are the same and every diagnosis of epilepsy has a different trail to full recovery. The recoveries will be different, but most of all, the life can be an Adventure!

# MY ADVANTAGE IS YOU

By David W. Stendel

I took advice from a worthy friend

When I questioned what I should do…

He said, "My son, many things are soon to change

And it's to your advantage too…."

Yet, for quite some time I've been waiting; debating

Trying to live a better life

Lord, when there's no doubt about

The way life should go- Oh, I know

My Advantage Is You


Why it hadn't happened sooner?

I haven't got a clue

But now my life's getting better and better, Lord

Now that my advantage is you!

Please keep me away from the evil ways

And make my life safe from sin. . . .

I know there's been times when prayer has

slipped my mind

And I'm not saying it won't happen again. . .

Just keep me closer – Lord, closer to you

Giving me confidence in all that I do

'Cause when there's no doubt about the

 Way life should go

Lord, I know my advantage is you!


Why it hadn't happened sooner

I haven't got a clue

But now my life's getting better and better, Lord

Knowing My Advantage Is You. . . .{repeat}

David W. Stendel

# ABOUT THE AUTHOR

David W. Stendel was born in Manistee, Michigan, and diagnosed with epilepsy at age 9. The misunderstanding of epilepsy made growing up quite a task, but the accomplishments of writing songs, stories, poems, and fictional novels, gave him a strike of confidence.

Knowing that many others fight the same burdens of epilepsy today, David decided to give other epileptics the chance to learn from his experiences. Today, after 45 years of dealing with epilepsy, David lives in Traverse City, Michigan, and is proud of all he does and all he has achieved. He believes any person can achieve his or her goals, even though some may have larger "blockades" to jump. David is an avid outdoorsman with a love of hunting and fishing, but he also spends a lot of time working on another "blockade."

Made in the USA
Lexington, KY
16 April 2018